I Blame the Beatles

The End of an Era

Tom Widdicombe

GW00566763

Published by
Cottage Publishing
72 Fore Street
Bovey Tracey
Newton Abbot
Devon TQ13 9AE
Tel: (01626) 835757
Fax: (01626) 835758

ISBN 1 897785 089

Line Drawings - Henry Widdicombe
Cover Illustration - David Hart
Editor - Sarah Widdicombe

Printed by
Moor Print, Manaton, Devon

Credit where credit is due

My thanks to George Robertson, editor of the *Mid-Devon Advertiser*, for publishing my letters and the many replies to them. It is down to George that we have all been able to have such a good laugh. Sadly, his home is shortly to be demolished when construction of the moorland motorway system commences (see map). Doesn't it make you wonder if there is any justice in this world at all?

My thanks also to my daughter Frances for design and layout, my son Henry for the drawings, and David for the cover illustrations.

And finally, my thanks to the Moretonhampstead Traffic Group, for unwittingly supplying the inspiration for the now infamous Haytor Traffic Group. May I put it on record, with all sincerity, that I fully accept that there is a genuine traffic problem in and around Moretonhampstead.

Dear Reader

It is surely no coincidence that the decline of the Conservative Party over the last two years has been more than matched by the growth, in global terms, of the Haytor Traffic Group. Starting from humble beginnings, with nothing more than a simple desire to improve traffic conditions in and around Haytor, over the last few months the Group has taken on huge economic and sociological significance, not only in the Teignbridge area but also throughout many parts of the South Hams.

As chairman of the Group, and consequently at the heart of this ever more ambitious organisation, it is my great honour to present to you this small volume of letters which chronicle what has become a hitherto unparalleled event in the history of our magnificent nation.

We will undoubtedly look back on 1997 as a turning point for the British people. Will we ever understand how, or indeed why, the most sophisticated electorate on the face of this earth have rejected what has surely been the most successful government this country has ever known, and yet at the same time have wholeheartedly embraced the Haytor Traffic Group? Can anyone believe that John Major and myself, two men from such humble beginnings who until now have shared similar successes in the world of public service, have now experienced such contrasting fortunes? As John retires into obscurity, to his world of memoirs and cricket, I find myself at the helm of one of the fastest-growing and most influential movements of the late twentieth century.

I have given much thought to this phenomenon over the last few months, and even now I am not sure I fully understand the reasons behind this extraordinary mass movement in conciousness. Is there a simple one-word answer? I somehow doubt it. It is my humble wish that perhaps through the pages of this book, you the reader will begin to understand the full significance of these momentous events.

Thank you all for your support over the last couple of years, and remember: the Haytor Traffic Group belongs to you, the people, and will, as always, be used exclusively for my own profit wherever and whenever possible.

Tom Widdicombe (Chairman, Haytor Traffic Group)

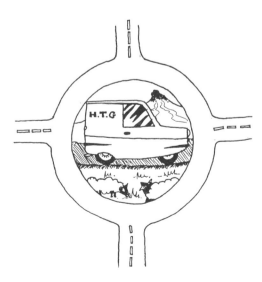

*From
a
single
letter
an
empire
grew....*

These personalities all wore school ties

SIR: Hats off to South Dartmoor Community College for excluding a twelve-year-old girl because she won't wear a tie. What a relief it is that our educational establishments are at last taking a stand against such subversive behaviour.

In my day, we all had to wear caps as well as ties, and 'short back and sides' was mandatory, too. The youngsters of today should take a long, hard look at the results of such good, old-fashioned discipline, and then they will realise how important tie-wearing really is.

Just looking at some of the more recent of our country's leading figures, it is so clear that both family values and good, honest business standards are dependant on wearing a tie as a child.

Prince Charles, Mark Thatcher, Cecil Parkinson, Alan Clarke, David Mellor, Sir Jeffrey Archer, Jonathan Aitken, David Tredinnick, Sir Gerry Wiggins – these are just a few of the many people who wore ties as children.

Yes, I blame the Beatles for the sorry state our country is in today. The sooner we all get our ties on and follow the example set by the good, honest, upright citizens named above the better it will be for all of us.

TOM WIDDICOMBE,
Woodlands,
Haytor Vale,
Newton Abbot.

He blames The Beatles!

SIR: So here we go again: just because the boss of the national lottery, on an annual salary of £240,000, gets a bonus of a further £120,000, out come all the whingers.

For goodness sake, the man is doing a good job; Camelot's profits are well above projections and their shareholders can all look forward to healthy dividends.

On top of that, don't forget the enormous benefits of the lottery for the ordinary man in the street.

In the last month alone the lottery has given Winston Churchill jnr., MP, £12 million for some letters and speeches that were vital to maintaining the quality of our lives. That was followed up with an £80 million donation to the British film industry;surely no-one can deny the difference that will make to us all.

The sooner we all stop moaning and, following the example of our government, get our snouts in the trough, the better it will be for all of us.

Yes, I blame the Beatles. All that nonsense about caring for other people and making a world that is a pleasure for us all to live in.

Just remember, you can go and read those speeches any time you want, and it's all because of the national lottery and its hard-working boss.

TOM WIDDICOMBE,
Woodlands,
Haytor Vale,
Newton Abbot.

21 JUNE 1995

TOM WIDDICOMBE,
   WOODLANDS,
      HAYTOR VALE,
         NEWTON ABBOT.

SOME 'ORDINARY' PEOPLE COULD NOT EARN
£240,000 IN A LIFETIME, BUT THAT'S
ALRIGHT ISN'T IT BECAUSE IT KEEPS PEOPLE
LIKE YOU WHERE YOU ARE AND THE 'RIFF-
RAFF' IN THEIR PLACE.
LET'S HOPE THE LOCAL PEOPLE DON'T
THINK HAYTOR AND THE VALE IS FULL
OF PEOPLE LIKE YOU.

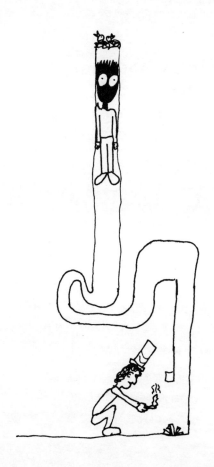

*"This will teach
the little so and so
to get stuck"*

Still blames The Beatles!

SIR: Well done, Patrick Nicholls, for voting in the House of Commons last week in favour of cutting Devon County Council's education budget.

It is indeed high time that a stand was made against the 'something for nothing' society that we live in, and who better to lead the way than our local MP?

Surely everybody knows by now that if you want to give your children a decent education then you will need to get out your cheque-books and send them to one of England's many excellent public schools.

This way, not only do you avoid the overcrowded classes and crumbling buildings used by the less well off, but you provide a ready-made network of middle class acquaintances which will be invaluable to your children in later life.

Oh, how I yearn for those good old days, when the ordinary people were grateful to be taught to read the Bible and sign their names on lifetime contracts of employment.

Believe me, only this Government has the will and the desire to turn the clocks back to those glorious times.

If I have only one regret about central heating, it must be the loss of so many chimneys, the cleaning of which could provide so much employment for so many young children.

Yes, I blame the Beatles and the Sixties for propagating the ridiculous notion that we could create a civilized society of well-educated people enjoying and sharing the fruits of this wonderful creation.

TOM WIDDICOMBE,
Woodlands,
Haytor Vale,
Newton Abbot.

Beatles brought more pleasure than the Government...

SIR: I thought I had to write after reading with interest comments written by Tom Widdicombe in your paper, Friday, June 23.

He seems a bitter man with nothing better to do than run the younger generation down, also have digs at the Beatles and the Sixties.

The Beatles brought music, and pleasure, to thousands of people of all ages, whereas the Government he supports has done nothing for the last fifteen years except bring misery and mass unemployment to millions of people.

Not everyone can get out a cheque-book and pay for their children to go to a public school. If everyone could send their children to a public school, then those too would become overcrowded. He should remember over the years plenty of ordinary people have done well in life.

As for his remarks about it being a pity there are not more chimneys where children could be employed to clean them. That is inhuman. Does he not realise that hundreds of children died doing that job, also as young as nine, crippled in mills, etc, so owners could make vast amounts of money and pay hardly any wages.

Perhaps he never had children, he might think differently, but I doubt it very much. Also under this Government no-one can sign life-time contracts of employment, the reason being there is no work.

But I could see Tom Widdicombe in a three-cornered hat in charge of a workhouse, making sure no youngster has a second helping of gruel. All so sad he was never young himself.

M. C. PARKER,
6 Shute Hill Crescent,
Teignmouth.

We suspect there was much tongue-in-cheek about Tom Widdicombe's letter. Another, on the subject of the pay rise for the managing director of South West Water, is printed below – Ed.

SWW pay rise will make Britain great again...

SIR: For goodness sake, let's jolly well keep things in perspective regarding the 45 per cent rise in salary for the managing dirtector of South West Water.

The poor man has done a magnificent job for the shareholders. He has maximised profits, using the age-old combination of exhorbitant charges in return for minimal services.

Furthermore, he has had the advantage, given to him by this Government, of a monopoly situation, and so has not had to worry about competition from other suppliers.

Virtually any member of the Conservative Party would be able to tell us that water is indeed the ideal commodity to market. There is no choice for the consumer, water privatisation is a businessman's dream come true. 'Pay up or die of thirst'.

I really cannot believe that anyone would be cynical enough to imagine that the paymasters of the Tory Party are grabbing what they can now, just in case the bubble bursts at the next general election.

Remember, this Government has generously offered the nurses a guaranteed one per cent pay rise, and only this week has come up with an offer of three per cent for the train drivers which, with inflation at 3.25 per cent, is only a small cut in pay.

Yet again, I have to blame the Beatles for the way old-fashioned values are dwindling in our society.

A one per cent rise for those people looking after the sick, a cut in wages for those people working on the railways, and a 45 per cent rise for someone who can make a huge profit out of a captive market. Surely these are the values that will make Britain great again?

TOM WIDDICOMBE,
Woodlands,
Haytor Vale,
Newton Abbot.

Won't water down his views on The Beatles

SIR: Brown tap water, dirty beaches, sewage in the sea, massive pay rises to its directors, coupled with ever-rising water bills – South West Water and all that is wrong with it, that is all we ever hear about in the papers these days.

I am sure I speak for the majority when I say I am heartily sick of all this criticism of this well-meaning and caring company.

Let's try looking at the good points for a change. For example, no-one ever talks about the lovely new modern. logo painted on the side of SWW vehicles, and then there is the colour of the vans, that's very nice, too.

I personally doubt that any state-owned enterprise would ever have had the vision to come up with such an attractive design. I do think it is so important to present a good image to the public; never forget the oft-quoted adage, presentation is all.

I can't help feeling that the people of this country are too quick to complain. Why, I can remember way back before the Beatles ever had a single hit, we would be grateful to get water out of our taps, whatever the colour. As for sewage in the sea, we all thought it was great fun.

Yes, I am afraid that thirteen years of Thatcherism has not been enough to re-instil the John Bull spirit into the once-great British public. Who would have thought that a pop group from Liverpool could have such a devastating effect on the psyche of an entire nation.

TOM WIDDICOMBE,
Woodlands,
Haytor Vale.

Motorway spur to access Widecombe-in-the-Moor?

SIR: How disappointed I was to see our local MP, Patrick Nicholls, come out against the proposed motorway extension from Exeter to Plymouth.

I do hope that what I presume is no more than a belated attempt to court local opinion as the election draws near will not stand in the way of this much-needed development.

I look forward to the completion of this project in the near future as only then will the next phase, or what has locally become known as the hidden agenda, be seriously considered.

Yes, the long-awaited motorway spur from Drumbridges roundabout to Widecombe-in-the-Moor is now closer than ever to becoming a reality, and I think I speak for everyone when I say what a relief it will be when work finally begins on this vital part of our motorway network.

Only the local residents and the coach drivers will be able to tell you how annoying these picturesque country lanes can be, not to mention the endless sheep, horses and cows we have to put up with all over the roads.

I have calculated that myself, as an ordinary individual, on an average journey from my home to Trago Mills could save as much as three minutes. Using this as a guide, we can see that the advantages to local businesses would be enormous.

Of course, there are other advantages too. Most of the route is through uninhabited wasteland, so there shouldn't be too much trouble with the nimby factor.

Then, of course, there is the ample supply of local materials which, once the spur is completed, could be used for motorway construction elsewhere in the country.

Lastly, the area above Haytor Vale itself is ideal for a service station which, as well as serving the extra tourists that would surge into the area, would provide much-needed local employment.

Enough of this 'Strawberry Fields Forever' mentality, we only have to look at towns like Bracknell, Swindon and Milton Keynes to see what can be achieved by keeping an open mind to progress and development.

TOM WIDDICOMBE,
Woodlands,
Haytor Vale,
Newton Abbot.

Multi-storey car park idea for visitors to Widecombe

SIR: I speak on behalf of just about all the residents of Widecombe-in-the-Moor, when I say what a jolly good laugh we all had at Tom Widdicombe's letter of August 11 re: Motorway spur to access Widecombe-in-the-Moor.

It was the funniest letter to have been published for ages. But why, we wonder, does Mr Widdicombe's idea of paradise stop at a mere service station over Haytor Vale?

Had he not thought of a beautiful multi-storey car park on the top of Widecombe hill, or how about a few superstores in some of the boring green fields?

To hell with the cattle and sheep, who needs them? The farmers can all go into B&B, or turn their hands to other trades.

As for the ponies on the moor, they can all be carted off to the slaughter houses for pet food.

We could have a tremendous leisure complex in the heart of the village, but we would have to demolish St Pancreas Church. Well, it's been there for several hundred years or so, time it was pulled down.

A couple of large housing estates would be nice, and even the odd tower-block doted around would add to the overall picture.

We could do away with the village post office (Sorry Mike and Jenny, but that's progress) and have a burger bar and all-night amusement arcade to give the youngsters something to do.

The village green could be an outdoor swimming pool, or an indoor market.

We could have discos, night-clubs, maybe even a cinema. The possibilities are endless.

No-one ever comes to visit Widecombe these days, after all, what's here? A handful of crumbling old cottages, lanes choked with animals, and all this dreadful greenery! So the influx of tourists would be good for us, too. Get us out of our country bumpkin ways.

Yes, Mr Widdicombe certainly had us laughing here in our 'strawberry fields' and made us all aware of what we are missing out on in life.

We appreciated his letter so much, we may even begin a collection fund in his honour. We'll call it the 'Send Mr Widdicombe to Bracknell, Swindon or Milton Keynes fund', and if Mr Widdicombe were ever to visit us out here in our stone-age settlements, we have a few suggestions to put to him, too!

JENNY WREN,
Bonehill,
Widecombe-in-the-Moor.

Advertiser/Post **Friday, August 18, 1995**

Tom could choke!

SIR: If correspondent Tom Widdicombe keeps his tongue in his cheek much longer he will choke himself.

HARRY
HAYTOR.
(address supplied).

Mr Widdicombe is only kidding, honest

Sir: I would like to give my view on a letter sent into your paper Friday August 11 concerning the new motorway spur from Drumbridge's Roundabout to Widecombe-in-the-Moor.

Of course, sent in by the man who does not like The Beatles, Mr Tom Widdicombe.

I was very pleased that local MP Patrick Nicholls had come out against the proposed motorway extension, and I'm not a Tory.

Visitors come to Devon to see the moor, even park and walk up those country lanes that Tom Widdicombe wants to see destroyed.

Fields, country lanes, moors, etc., is what England is all about. I'm for progress, but not for ripping the countryside to pieces, so people can save three minutes to go to Trago Mills.

Also, animals often wander down lanes because people go in fields and leave gates open, and most local people love the country lane walks, etc.

Perhaps Tom Widdicombe lives local, but is not local-born he then might think different.

To finish, I would like to use a song by The Beatles: most people prefer Penny Lane, than Penny Motorways.

M. C. PARKER,
6 Shute Hill Crescent
Teignmouth.

Relieved by US purchase of SWEB

I have to confess that I do not fully understand the workings of the global market, but I am sure I can relax in the knowledge that Mrs Thatcher, all those years ago, knew what she was doing when she sold the electricity companies back to the people.

Regrettably I, along with the majority of the population, didn't have any spare cash at the time, and so were unable to take advantage of her generous offer.

However, those that were fortunate enough to buy their share of SWEB can now cash in fourfold. Yes, this is the joy of the capitalist system, if you are rich, for no apparent reason, you get richer.

If you are poor, just think, now when you turn on the light the profit made from selling you the electricity that you use goes all the way to America. Isn't that amazing?

At least we can relax in the comforting knowledge that it is now the Americans that are responsible for providing our electricity.

And, of course, the Germans and the Japanese are responsible for providing our cars, not forgetting the notable exception of the Reliant Robin, the flagship of our very own British industry. How my heart swells with pride when I see one making it's steadfast way along our ever-expanding road system.

Yes, I think we have a lot to thank this Government for. With their skilful economic guidance, massive unemployment and total rejection of a minimum wage rate, propped up by a state-funded income support policy, they have have supplied the world with a ready source of cheap labour.

It all reminds me of my school days; 11 o'clock on a Monday morning, singing together on the Home service, or was it the Light programme?, that wonderful line from the stirring old ditty 'Rule Brittania' – incidentally, not written by the Beatles – 'Britains never, never, never shall be slaves.'

TOM WIDDICOMBE,
Woodlands,
Haytor Vale.

PUT NATIONAL PRIDE ASIDE

SIR: Tom Widdicombe rejoices in the fact that the Americans are now responsible for providing our electricity – and I agree with him. With all their experience, they should be able to ensure that our electricity is cheaper, and the service better, than the old SWEB Board provided.

But they're not British, he will say! Well, I remember what a disaster Jaguar was under British management, and what a triumph it is now the Americans own it. Perhaps the Yanks can do the same for SWEB.

The point is this. If British workers can make good cars or computers or TV sets or even electricity, but British owners and managers can't organise an efficient business for them, then let's welcome the Japanese and Germans and Americans who can. If foreigners are better at managing manufacturing industry than we are, then let them come here and do it.

I think the British are big enough to admit they can't do everything superbly. In the end, we get the jobs and the export earnings. They get a few dividends for their trouble.

This is what the global market, which Mr Widdicombe admits he doesn't understand, is all about. The Americans come here and make cars and electricity and computers. Over in the States, Shell produces a lot of petrol, ICI makes a lot of paint, Hanson mines a lot of coal, and so on.

As a result, Britain is the largest foreign investor in America, and our investments there are almost exactly equal to theirs in Britain. We are each, therefore, doing the things we are best at in each other's countries. And we are all better off as a result.

Better some good American jobs in Britain, I suggest, than a lot of national pride, but nothing to eat!

PETER WILLS,
Far Horizons,
Haytor.

Another one down to The Beatles

SIR: My thanks to Peter Mills (Letters, September 29) for his clear explanation of how the global market works and why it is to the benefit of us all.

I must say I look forward to the extra jobs that he assures us will be created by the takeover of SWEB by Southern Electric USA.

I cannot believe that I was so politically naive as to imagine that the American company purchased SWEB because it was a seriously undervalued, already profitable company supplying a huge captive market who have no choice but to buy their product.

No, of course, that is not the reason for this takeover or indeed any other takeover, this is all about making things better for you and me, the consumer.

Did you know that these large global companies have special research departments scanning the world to see how and where they can best improve the lot of the people?

Yes, that is their prime concern, our welfare.

They are not there to feather their own nests, the huge salaries and share options are merely a happy by-product of pursuing their true goal, wealth and happiness for everyone.

So, as the world appears to lurch uncontrollably towards its destiny of eternal progress towards material fulfilment, let's all relax and breath easy in the knowledge that our future lies in the hands of such well-known philanthropists as Rupert Murdoch, Lord Hanson, Jonathan Aitken, Tiny Rowland and all.

I can only blame the immortal words of John Lennon's classic song *Power to the People* for the inability of so many people to accept such obvious and simplistic logic.

Surely, if there is one thing we all must have learnt' over the last sixteen years, it is to trust the market place.

At home we now have people without jobs sleeping on pavements, and abroad we are destroying the rainforests to produce beefburgers for the world markets; still, it makes a profit so it must be right.

TOM WIDDICOMBE,
Woodlands,
Haytor Vale.

Give it a rest!

SIR: Is it not about time that we readers had a rest from the likes of your more-than-regular contributions from the Brinicombe and Widdcombe, et al, pontificating on whatever subject they wish to bore us with?

They have no relevance in today's world, please put them out to pasture, preferably together so that they can bore the pants off each other.

BOB BRUCE,
Oakdene,
Woodland,
Ashburton.

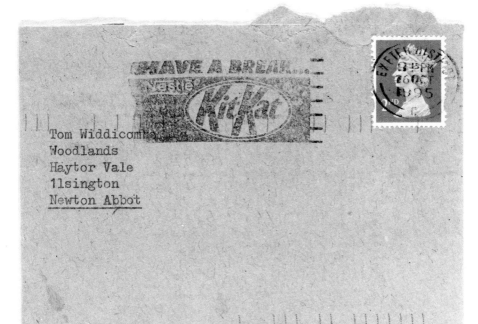

Tom Widdicombe
Woodlands
Haytor Vale
Ilsington
Newton Abbot

Who let you out?

Sorry for the upset

SIR: I am sorry that I seem to have upset one of your readers with my letters, that I have conscientiously written and submitted to the *MDA*.

At the same time I feel this gentleman from 'Woodland' has read into my letter quite a different tone, and I feel an explanation would help.

All the letters I have submitted have been of a topical nature, and day-to-day interests.

Can I say that I am far from living in the past, this can only ever be a follow-up to a previous correspondent as being supportive.

It is quite obvious that at my age I have, thank goodness, acquired the knowledge and experience of the past, which enables me to draw comparisons when writing about topical things.

Life has to go on for all of us, some are modernists, some are traditionalists, and others are for the 'Good Old Days', so what is wrong with a compromise?

L. BRINICOMBE (MR),

**White Gate,
64 Abbotsbury Road,
Newton Abbot.**

Free press and free speech is the right of every citizen

SIR: Unlike Mr Brinicombe, I will not apologise for taking advantage of the letters page of this newspaper to express my views on matters I consider worthy of comment.

The free press and freedom of speech in this country is something we should all be proud of, and it is the right of every citizen to hold forth whenever they feel the need.

Personally, I do feel that such topics as the possibility of a foreign takeover bid for that great British flagship, the Reliant Robin, or the issue of the underlying hostility in the local community towards the proposed motorway to Widecombe are indeed matters of great relevance to today's world and our local community.

My advice to Mary Whitehouse is, if you don't like what is on the telly, turn if off. Similarly, I can only suggest to 'the gentleman from Woodland', if he finds he is bored by a letter he is reading, stop reading it.

This simple little tip, which I have to say I have been using since birth, will, hopefully, allow him to enjoy his life to the full, regardless of other people's points of view.

In the meantime Mr Brinicombe, if you've got something to say, say it. Myself, I don't remember reading any of your letters anyway (but then you probably don't remember reading any of mine).

> **TOM WIDDICOMBE,**
> Woodlands,
> Hayter Vale.

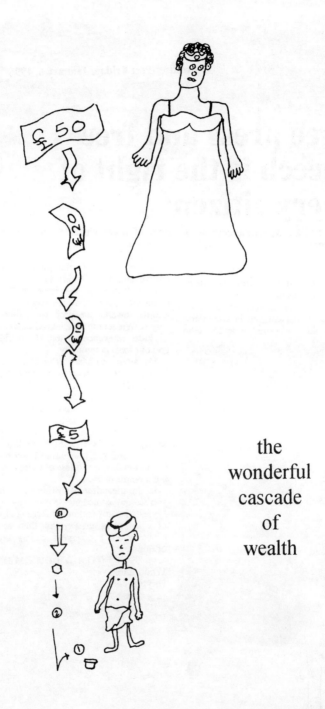

the
wonderful
cascade
of
wealth

...rushing to his defence

SIR: As a lifelong potential Tory voter, yet again I feel compelled to rush to the defence of our beleaguered MP, Mr Patrick Nicholls.

Just because he was elected by us to serve the people of this constituency in parliament, is that any reason to start having a go at him because he might have used his privileged position for possible gain?

Of course, as mere men and women in the street, it is understandable that many of us fall into the trap of believing that parliamentary time and money should be used to deal with matters of national interest rather than to give MPs the opportunity of feathering their own nests.

Yes, an easy mistake to make and over the years one that I have made myself many times – indeed, often it looks like all that Tory MPs are inter-ested in are their own bank balances.

I know that, sometimes, especially in situations like this, it is all too easy to imagine that the Tory doctrine of self-help is a convenient cover-up for selfish greed, but please, let's not be so cynical. Remember, the creation of that wealth then filters down through society and, yes, everyone gets richer and richer. It is a wonderful system of such beauty it almost brings tears to my eyes.

May I, through the columns of this excellent newspaper, take the opportunity to wish everyone a happy and prosperous new year, and let us always remember the life of the master, Mr Peter Cook, who, it is said, steadfastly refused to take anything seriously, ever.

TOM WIDDICOMBE,
Woodlands,
Haytor Vale.

PRIMARY ROUTE ROAD IS SIMPLY A DISGRACE!

SIR: With reference to your correspondent last week complaining about the appalling conditions of the A382 Bovey Tracey to Whiddon Down road, I am sure that your readers would like to know it is designated by Devon County Council as a primary county route!

Furthermore, this road is also regarded in the Devon 2011 Structure Plan as part of the 'high-quality road network', enabling it to support the trans-European networks.

We just wonder who is kidding who?

The road is a disgrace, and should be improved immediately, or through heavy goods vehicles banned from using it.

The Devon 2011 Structure Plan consultation draft is available for all to read in local libraries.

B. C. STADDON,
Chairman,
Moretonhampstead
Traffic Group

c/o Pitt House,
Ford Street,
Moretonhampstead

Six-lane highway to Moretonhampstead!

SIR: How delighted I am to see that the subject of road development in the National Park has once again resurfaced on the letters page.

After the largely positive response to my plan first disclosed in this very newspaper, to construct a motorway from Drumbridges to Widecombe-on-the-Moor, perhaps I could suggest another even more obvious alternative.

Using a six-lane highway to allow for future growth, we could build an orbital system through Bovey, up the Wray valley to Moretonhampstead, and then out on the Princetown road to just past the pony centre. Then along Long Lane, past Hound Tor and then, at Hexworthy Gate we could have a spur off to Widecombe and the main ring road could come back past Haytor Rocks and drop back down into Bovey.

This plan will alleviate all our local traffic problems which, let's face it, are beginning to make Hyde Park Corner look like Toytown. Yes, only the other day I met two cars on my way to Ashburton.

It will also allow visitors to complete a convenient circuitous tourist route of the moor in less than half an hour, including a five-minute drive up the Wray valley, described in the guide books as one of

the most beautiful valleys in Britain.

They will also have good views of Houndtor and Haytor with, of course, the option of a quick and easy diversion into Widdicombe if they can spare the time.

Anyone who is worried about the short term inconvenience of this admittedly ambitious development need fear not. All the raw materials needed will give us a once and for ever opportunity to get rid of all these unsightly stone walls that have been littering the moor for centuries.

As for the service station on Haytor Down, I have had a word with my mate Dave from the Mobil garage and he says he would be more than happy to run it if

someone would build it for him. I reassured him that no doubt there would be an EEC grant to cover that.

I hope these proposals meet with the approval of the More-tonhampstead Traffic Group, and indeed the people whose houses will sadly have to be knocked down to allow construction to commence. I am sure they will understand that it is, in the end, for the greater good. After all, let us not overlook the hidden truth in the age old adage: 'Speed is essential, time is money.'

All the best.

TOM
WIDDICOMBE,
Woodlands,
Haytor Vale,
Newton Abbot.

Advertiser/Post **Friday, March 29, 1996**

"I am living proof of the maxim that if you want a job done, you give it to a busy man."

The Teignbridge MP was nominated for his services to public life by members of the Worshipful Company of Masons and the Worshipful Company of Feltmakers.

"I pay more in tax each year than I receive in my parliamentary pay packet"

Political forum

TEIGNBRIDGE MP, Patrick Nicholls has declined to attend a public meeting tonight, organised by South Devon Real World

He is losing money!

SIR: I read with mixed feelings Patrick Nicholls' making a virtue of necessity. I now know that he is selflessly honouring the people of Teignbridge by being their MP.

He is, in fact, losing money. Greater love hath no man.

Obviously, MPs should not receive pay increases, but take money from various firms, or institutions who, heaven forbid, should have an ulterior motive in employing him thus.

After reading his self-justifying article, he left me with a strong feeling. Yes, I felt like leaving the room and throwing up!

J. CHESTERMAN,

**Dawlish Road,
Teignmouth.**

From a long-time supporter of our MP!

SIR: As a long-time supporter of our somewhat jaded local MP Mr Patrick Nicholls, how my heart sank when I read his article attempting to justify his income of £90,000 plus a year.

What better way to start up endless correspondence about a subject he would surely prefer we would all forget about?

The great mass of ordinary people in this country are happy enough to serve the rich and famous but, please, Patrick, don't rub their noses in it as well.

If you are lucky enough to make thousands of pounds out of your power and influence then surely it is best to keep quiet about it if you possibly can?

Take it from me, I know people who are working their butts off for less than £10,000 a year, and then they are taxed on that.

I also know people who don't have jobs, not because they don't want to work but because this economic system needs high unemployment to keep inflation down.

These people have to bring up their families on less money per week than Princess Di spends on breakfast at her favourite restaurant.

Now, I know you can argue that as long as there are more haves than have-nots then what the hell, we'll win the election anyway; but a bit of sensitivity is surely not too much to ask for?

I just don't think it really helps if people think their MP is coining it in for doing nothing.

In fact, I have even heard it said that if MPs didn't occupy their time with so many outside business interests they could give more attention to the real world where most of us live. I don't know, they'll be asking for cake next.

TOM WIDDICOMBE,
Woodlands,
Haytor Vale.

Woodlands
Haytor Vale
Newton Abbot
Devon
TQ13 9XR

Tel: 01364 661470
Email: tom@mail.zynet.co.uk

23rd June 96

Dear Editor

I am enclosing another copy of my last letter which I delivered by hand to your office on 11th June. I am only doing this because the one other time I delivered a letter by hand it didn't appear in print for about ten weeks after I wrote it. Sensitive being that I am I was convinced that my number was up and that yet again the people of mid-Devon would be reduced to a diet of humourless diatribes.

Of course, I fully accept your editorial judgement and you may think my last letter is not up to scratch. Personally I think it is one of my more inspired pieces and I would be greatly disappointed if my ever-growing fan club were denied the opportunity of reading it. Either way, may I take this chance to thank you for giving me the time of day over the last year or so and I hope your worthy journal may long continue to flourish.

All the Best

Tom Widdicombe

More about the Wray Valley motorway

SIR: As the person who had the unfortunate task of breaking the news of the highly-controversial proposals for the Wray Valley motorway, I do feel in some way responsible for the alarming drop in property prices in and around the charming village of Lustleigh.

Yet again, innocent people are paying the price of progress.

Plummet

How I feel for these decent, honest citizens; people who have probably voted Conservative all their lives, who have moved into the country only to find that they now live within a hundred yards of a proposed six-lane highway.

Consequently, they now see the value of their homes plummeting.

However, I now have some news which will help us all through these difficult times. As chairman of the Haytor Traffic Group, I was recently in conversation with the chairman of the Channel Tunnel Company, the Right Honourable Sir Andy Borehole.

He informed that me, following the huge financial success of the channel tunnel, negotiations are now well under way for the construction of a six-lane tunnel from Bovey Tracey to Moreton-hampstead, thus offering a solution to one of the most pressing problems of our times.

Pixies

What really impressed me about the new proposals was the lengths that the company has gone to in order to make the project a total success.

For example, if anybody is worrying about what is going to happen to all the stuff they take out of the hole, fear not. A deal has already been done with the Dartmoor Pixie Centre.

All the waste will be reconstituted into little pixies and sold to the millions of extra tourists who will be able to visit the area because of the vast improvement in journey times.

Yet another remarkable innovation that is surely a first for Devon.

Modern technology has enabled the tunnel to include a series of periscopes which will allow tourists to enjoy the valley in all its glory without wasting valuable time negotiating the tricky bends of the existing road.

You may well be wondering how on earth the national park will ever give permission for such an innovative feat of engineering?

Amazingly, nothing has been left to chance, and the company have been assured that the park will give full support to the project as long as the entrance to the tunnel in no way detracts from the beautiful architecture of the new golf centre that now graces the skyline to the north of the town and, of course, all external woodwork must be stained in dark oak.

TOM WIDDICOMBE,
Woodlands,
Haytor Vale.

Graph to illustrate the amount of time that will be saved after the construction of the M909, using Trago Mills as the most common destination.

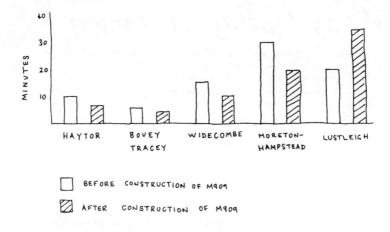

From this graph you can work out how much you personally will save in cash every time you make this journey. For example, using the suggested minimum wage of £4.20 per hour (7p per minute), from Haytor to Trago I can save myself an incredible 3 minutes, or in financial terms, 21p. Of course, the longer the distance that you have to travel, the greater the savings will be.

Sadly, the one anomaly is the charming village of Lustleigh. Because of unforeseen technical difficulties, the Lustleigh interchange in the Wray Valley was, to put it simply, just too expensive. This now means that Lustleigh residents will have to join the M909 at Moretonhampstead, adding approximately fifteen minutes to their journey time. Regrettably, this will undoubtedly further depress the already falling house prices in and around that area.

DON'T EVER FORGET:
SPEED IS ESSENTIAL, TIME IS MONEY!

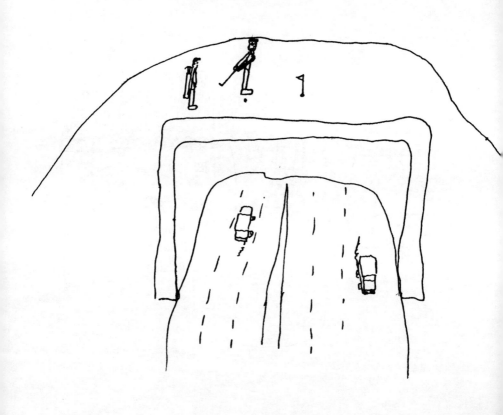

Wrey Valley tunnel would benefit another type of driver!

SIR: I write regarding Tom Widdicombe's last letter, in this newspaper's July 5 edition, concerning the Wray Valley motorway.

I am pleased to see that, at long last, a sensible proposal to the traffic problems along the Bovey Tracey-to-Moretonhampstead road has been voiced and, by the sounds of it, are well under way to fruition.

I was pleased also to note that the project was in no way to detract from the new golf driving range, but wonder if all aspects of the proposed tunnel have been thoroughly considered from the golfer's point of view?

Having a tunnel entrance in the close proximity of the driving range is, of course, undoubtedly a very prudent move on behalf of the planners, giving the range an even more 'true-to-the-golf-course' feel, having a hole to aim for.

Has, though, for example, consideration been given to a flag being incorporated into the tunnel entrance arch, thus giving drivers (both of vehicles and balls) a far greater chance of getting down the hole in one?

Has also consideration been given to one, or maybe two, bunkers, either side of the entrance? These could double as escape routes for the drivers of vehicles whose brakes fail on the way down into the tunnel.

Perhaps, if funds permit, one of the A38 water hazards could also be relocated to just in front of the tunnel, thus enhancing the range still further, whilst also providing a means of calming any would-be speeders into the tunnel.

Perhaps at your next meeting with Sir Andy Borehole, Tom, due consideration could be given to the above suggestions.

In the meantime, my congratulations to the Haytor Traffic Group for getting this long overdue problem moving.

**KEVIN HARRISON,
5 Musket Road,
Heathfield,
Newton Abbot.**

A novel way of playing golf...!

SIR: I would like to reassure Mr Harrison and any other golf fans that this week I have been in conversation with my good friend Sir Andy Borehole, and he assures me that the welfare of the noble game is always uppermost in his mind. Indeed, the two great loves of his life are tunnelling and golf.

On many occasions he has said to me that even though he plays off a sixteen handicap, he always feels how much more convenient it would be for the players if the ball could travel from hole to hole via a tunnel rather than be whacked there by a stick.

Indeed, when Sir Andy first saw the golf range near the proposed entrance to the tunnel at Bovey Tracey, his comment was, what a fine agricultural barn it was. Imagine his delight when I told him it was, in fact, a golf range.

Like Mr Harrison, he immediately began to say how wonderful that golf and tunnelling should exist side by side in such harmony. Indeed, it is Sir Andy's greatest wish that one day the whole country, if not the whole world, will be covered with golf courses all linked together by huge tunnels, of course constructed by his ever more ambitious company.

Just to give you another indication of Sir Andy's devotion to the game, I must tell you about the first time I drove with him over the moor from my home in Haytor Vale down to Widecombe for a cream tea.

He simply could not believe that such a beautiful area was not a golf course. It was then that I explained to him about the National Park and the austere planning restrictions that they impose on the area.

The sight of Sir Andy, a man of truly great vision, standing by Haytor Rock against the Autumn sky will live with me forever. 'Never, ever, let this world be dictated to by little men in grey suits,' he said. 'One day, this whole area will be a golf course, you mark my words.'

As the words came out of his mouth I knew I was privileged to hear a great man speak. We walked back to the car in silence and I wondered if it would be months or years before his dreams began to manifest.

On a slightly different tack, I must thank everyone for the huge interest they have shown in the Haytor Traffic Group. Unfortunately, membership of this secret society is by invitation only but, because of the overwhelming importance of the Wrey Valley issue, I personally took the step of revealing the existence of this hitherto unknown group.

I can tell you now that I have done this at great cost to myself as I now face the prospect of expulsion from this society, bringing with it all the inconvenience and hardship faced by non-members. Alas, sometimes small sacrifices must be made for the greater good.

TOM WIDDICOMBE,
Woodlands,
Haytor Vale,
Newton Abbot.

Haytor Construction Company

est.1996

Directors: Tom Widdicombe
Sir Andy Borehole
Sir Tony Moorhouse
Ayam bin Cashari

PO Box 909
Ritz Hotel
Paris

10 September 1996

To: Teignbridge Highways Dept

Estimate to construct tunnel through the Wray Valley, and to supply and fit complete Motorway system as requested, including Dave's Service Station.

Labour	20,000,000,000
Materials, inc. dark oak woodstain	150,000,016
Optional on-site pixie manufacturing plant with drive-thru retail outlet	76,000,000
Removal of tunnel spoil to above site	54,000,000
Total	20,280,000,016

VAT <u>will</u> be charged if you can't pay cash (preferably up-front)

Schedule of work: In order to speed up the job, we will be hiring two diggers and will probably borrow an extra tractor and trailer or, quite frankly, it could take forever.

We trust this estimate will meet with your approval and look forward to hearing from you in the near future.

Yours faithfully

Miss Theresa Green, Secretary

- - - - - - - - - - snip here and shred on receipt -

PS Free, all expenses paid, foreign holidays in luxury hotels may be available to the entire finance department and their families.

This one is getting as carried away as Tom

SIR: It has taken me several weeks to tear myself away from staining the timber on my house dark brown and respond to Tom Widdicombe's heart-warming news about the proposed tunnel for the Wrey Valley.

As a logical extension of this admirable scheme, I am delighted to be able to announce to your readers the proposed construction of a network of tunnels under Dartmoor, with vast underground destinations where visitors can enjoy a virtual experience of the moor without having to leave their cars.

The possibilities of multi-media 'theme' parks have hardly been explored, and no doubt it will be possible to allow visitors to experience suitably modified versions of the balmy breezes, friendly wildlife and helpful bureaucracy to be encountered on the surface.

The European Commission is being approached for funds to enable this imaginative scheme to be progressed. Mr Widdicombe doubtless will be pleased to learn that Haytor itself is proposed as the first underground Virtual Dartmoor Experience.

Cream teas will be served to visitors in the comfort of their cars, and takeaway mementoes will include a free example of the precise colour of woodstain to be employed when constructing your virtual longhouse when you get back home to the relative safety of Surbiton.

**C. J. F. GETHIN,
Higher Pudsham,
Buckland-in-the-Moor,
Ashburton.**

DARK BROWN WOOD STAIN

Tom senses the election approaches

SIR: Now that Tony Blair and his minders have moved the Labour party to the right of the Conservatives, it is surely time for all of us loyal Tory voters to think seriously about which way we should vote at the next election.

Over the last seventeen years, we have come to understand the importance of our leaders saying and promising one thing and then, having achieved power, promptly doing the exact opposite.

For the sake of the country, I sincerely hope that should Labour win, they will also have no problem in jettisoning most of their policies posthaste.

May I make a plea to my fellow voters? If anyone ever says the issue is policies, not personalities, for goodness sake ignore them. Policies are ever-changing but the personalities — they are with us for the duration.

So what is on offer in Teignbridge? On one side we have Sue Dann. Come on Sue, do we really know you? Would you send your kids to a grammar school? Do you think people should be paid less than £3.40 an hour?

Why do you want to be an MP, is it the money, the power or the glory? Come out from behind your ever-changing manifesto and tell us what you really believe, but be careful — Tony is a politician and his views are guided by potential votes, say the wrong thing and you surely won't make the shadow cabinet.

And, on the other side, we have our very own Patrick Nicholls who, it has to be said, hasn't made a serious gaffe for what seems like ages. I wonder whether this is a deliberate policy because of the impending election, or whether, coincidently, he is going through a period of much-deserved good fortune.

I must say my concern with Patrick is that he has a bit too much on his plate. I do think six, or is it nine directorships, a law firm, a family and a parliamentary constituency must keep him quite busy.

I can sympathise myself, as I am in fact the co-organiser of the Haytor Lottery syndicate and that gets a bit much sometimes.

And then, of course, we must mention the other chap, I can't think of his name for the moment, but he is very concerned about the A38.

Yes, I'm with you on that one but why don't you share my concern over the Wrey Valley proposals, surely there has got to be a few votes there too?

So, come on you two hopefuls, let us see what you are really like, and come on, Patrick, let's have another gaffe. It's time you gave Stanley Chew something to really get his teeth into.

All the Best.

TOM WIDDICOMBE,
Woodlands,
Haytor Vale,
Newton Abbot.

Sue Dann seeks a fair society

SIR: I would like to take this opportunity to reply to Tom Widdicombe of Haytor, who last week suggested that policies no longer mattered to a political party, and that only the personalities within a political party really counted.

That may be the case for other political parties, but it is certainly not in the Labour Party.

I was selected by Labour Party members for the vision that I have for society. A society that is fair and just, a society that gives opportunity to all and a society that promises to look after the needy and disadvantaged.

I want everyone to have a decent roof over their head.

I want every child to have access to the best schools and further education.

I want everyone to have access to training or a job.

I want everyone to have the best in health care.

This can only be achieved in a fair society where money should not be able to buy privilege. No longer should the wealthiest ten per cent be getting richer whilst the bottom ten per cent get poorer.

We need an economy run for the many and not the few. We need to ensure that everyone, young and old, has a stake in society. We need to fund frontline public services, not wasteful bureaucracy.

So, there you are, Tom, one person cannot achieve all that, not even one like me with a wonderful personality! We need the Labour Party to address the balance between 'the haves' and 'the have nots', and to do that we do have the policies.

SUE DANN,
Prospective Parliamentary Candidate
Labour Teignbridge,
8 Seymour Road,
Newton Abbot.

Mid-Devon Advertiser

I'LL NOMINATE YOU!! (AS A LABOUR CANDIDATE)

BARRY.

Friday, August 23, 1996
Established 1863
Incorporating Mid Devon Times

30p

Newton Abbot, Ashburton, Bovey Tracey, Buckfastleigh, Chudleigh, Dawlish, Exeter

Moretonhampstead, Teignmouth, Torbay, Totnes and South Devon Tel: 01626 5566

Should Tom stand for Parliament?

SIR: Your newspaper is indeed fortunate to receive so many gems of wisdom from the renowned Haytor gem, Tom Widdicombe. I take them all most seriously.

May I suggest, however, if readers can bear it, that this savant turns away from your columns in order to seek fresh outlets for his enquiring, not to mention devious, mind?

Is he man enough to shed his cloak of anarchy and universal detraction and stand as parliamentary candidate for Teignbridge himself?

He would, of course, have to shed many of his important, and possibly lucrative, commitments in order to do this, but I am sure he would be willing to suffer so that we may all gain. If not from his success, then at least a more entertaining election campaign.

We need such men of principle who will let us know where they stand, especially in relation to the Beatles. If he refuses to take up my challenge, then I can only blame Gerald.

CONCERNED VOTER,
(Name and address supplied).

Policies before personalities

SIR: Regular readers of letters to your newspaper will realise that jokey Tom Widdicombe had his tongue wedged in his cheek last week.

With some humorous examples, he suggested that the personality of a General Election prospective candidate is more important than policy. On this basis, Sue Dann would definitely be our next MP!

On a serious note, we are responsible people and we do want to know the policies of each party, so that we can make our own decisions on how to vote.

Do we want the greed philosophy of the Conservatives, when even Mr Nicholls, MP, complains about the privatised SW Water handouts to its former director?

Or, do we want the decent social policies of the Labour Party, arising from a philosophy of fairness for everyone; for example its public pledge to take '250,000 under-25 year-olds off benefit and into work'?

Tom's query on schools is personal, but I understand that Mr Nicholls' children go to a boarding school and Mrs Dann's children go to local (good) state schools.

More to the point is the Labour pledge to cut class sizes and improve the educational standards of all children.

Well done, Tom. Even if I do not agree with you, your letter stirred a response.

**TED CLAPTON,
Lower Hole Farmhouse,
Bridford.**

Keep 'em coming, Tom

SIR: One of the great freedoms enjoyed by citizens of this country is the opportunity to express their views on almost any subject in the Letters Pages of newspapers, and your newspaper is clearly a champion of this liberty. However, editors normally heed and quietly apply certain conventions.

While defending your right to publish whatever you wish, Sir, I wonder if you now regret printing Ms Dann's blatant election address masquerading as a letter?

Surely, we are going to have a surfeit of politicians and their wiles over the next few months without their intruding into your hospitality? After all, they have their own rights and freedoms when it comes to getting their messages right into our homes.

On the other hand, it is to be hoped that you will continue to publish anything and everything from the pen of Tom Widdicombe, who has a special place in our affections, as the village eccentric.

P. E. HART,
Little Moretons,
Combeinteignhead,
Newton Abbot.

Sir Tony
Moorhouse

Tom may be too busy to become an MP

SIR: Imagine my surprise on returning from holiday to find that not only had my vegetable garden been given a severe going over by some farmer's wretched sheep, but there was also huge speculation in the press concerning my political future.

I am indeed flattered that some of your readers think I should discontinue my financially extremely unrewarding career as an occasional writer to your excellent letters page, in order to stand for parliament in the Teignbridge constituency.

I have to confess that this is indeed not an entirely new idea as it is something I briefly considered in my childhood when, more than thirty-five years ago, my father explained to me the workings of a civilised democracy.

Since that time, however, I have become less and less impressed by both the behaviour and effectiveness of politicians in general, and have even begun to wonder if they are of any benefit to anyone bar themselves.

However, the prospect of a well-paid job with the built-in facility of voting at will for lucrative pay rises, plus the obvious spin-offs of consultancies and directorships, is not something to be turned down without some thought.

Of course, my main concern is that if elected I will have to find someone trustworthy to take over my duties with the Haytor lottery syndicate. One thing I do think I would have to make clear from the start is that I have no intention of over-committing myself.

I have already mentioned my small vegetable patch, which can be quite time-consuming and then, of course, I have to feed my goldfish and my two koi carp every day as well, so you can see I am already quite busy.

Perhaps Mr Nicholls can help me with my other concern. Will the phone ever stop ringing? Why, even after just a couple of letters in the local press I have had Sir Tony Moorhouse on the phone asking if I can work towards a relaxation of the planning constraints in the national park.

He, apparently, has clients queuing up for building plots and he assures me, categorically, that they have no problem whatsoever with the ever more controversial dark oak stain ruling.

TOM
WIDDICOMBE,
Woodlands,
Haytor Vale,
Newton Abbot.

Tom has something to say about school dress rules

SIR: With the exclusion of a pupil in another part of Devon for wearing a skirt two inches above her knee, I am left wondering if any of our local schools are considering the introduction of a Moslem-style dress code to help the teachers who have problems coping with the sight of the female body.

In one country I once visited, the women were forced to cover even their eyes, presumably in an attempt to help men avoid temptation.

Whilst on the subject of education, I am greatly reassured to see that my local secondary school has introduced North Korean-style democracy to complement the North Korean-style uniforms now so proudly worn by the younger students.

As described in the first issue of its new magazine, The College Chronicle, the new code of conduct has been created through a 'democratic, co-operative and consultative' process.

In line with North Korean policy, only selected issues were up for discussion and the democracy involved does not appear to have included any voting rights for the students themselves, who just happen to be the people most affected by the policies.

At long last, we are witnessing a grass roots movement back to those glorious days of old when we, the humble masses, were content to fulfil the wishes of our leaders.

Yes, thank goodness our schools are at last taking it upon themselves to stamp on all this nonsense about personal freedom and the rights of the individual. God forbid that we should ever breed a population capable of thinking for themselves.

Imagine all those children having to cope with the responsibility of deciding what to wear every morning — and just who are these subversives who think they should be able to go the toilet whenever they need to?

Yes, never mind the Beatles — straight lines, smart jackets, and plenty of goose-stepping, that is the recipe for success in life. After all, it hasn't done the North Koreans any harm, has it?

All the best.

TOM WIDDICOMBE,
Woodlands,
Haytor Vale,
Newton Abbot.

Someone who takes Tom seriously

SIR: I see by reading your paper last week Tom Widdicombe decided to surface again, talking, as usual, a lot drivel.

Why do we want to dress our children in North Korean-style clothes? We are British. We have already lost a lot of our culture and customs, so why this?

As for personal freedom, he should meet widows and parents who lost husbands and sons in two wars, so that this country had freedom and a right to think for ourselves.

He should try living in a country where even in this age, there is NO freedom. And if those brave men who fought

and died for us then had lost the war, then he would have seen straight lines, smart jackets, etc, and plenty of goose-stepping all over this country, even this area, only it would have been

jackboots worn by stormtroopers of the German army doing the goose-stepping and no freedom, even for Tom Widdicombe to write his letters, silly as they are.

MR M.C. PARKER, 6 Shute Hill Crescent, Teignmouth.

MID DEVON COMPREHENSIVE

...oh dear, looks like he has an enemy

You and your pathetic sense of humour are the kind of thing that undermines our society.

You may not like our country but a lot of people do

Do yourself and everyone else a favour, just shut up and go away

A true patriot

This advice, delivered by hand, received with grateful thanks on the morning of October 6th.

...oh dear, looks like he has a friend

SIR: I am happy to be able to tell you that, responding to pressure from environmentalists, the plans for a motorway spur to Widecombe – which your paper has so often publicised – have been dropped.

The idea of replacing the road with a railway was considered, but discarded, as rail travel is noisy, dirty, unhygienic, expensive and unreliable.

Instead, an alternative, environmentally-friendly solution has been adopted. It is planned to build a canal.

This magnificent construction will start at Stover, soar over Drumbridges roundabout by aquaduct, (with a spur to Trago to enable people to undertake environmentally-friendly shopping), pass through Liverton and, in a series of some 50 to 80 locks, through Ilsington to Haytor.

From there it will follow the line of the road to Harefoot Cross, where another series of locks will take it down to Widecombe.

In order to preserve the environment, machinery will not be used to dig the canal.

Instead, there will be a force of 10,000 labourers with spades and wheelbarrows, creating much-needed employment in the West Country.

In view of the contribution they have made to the debate, jobs will first be offered to road protesters, though it is feared they will be much too busy to have time to engage in gainful employment.

**P. WILLS,
2 Wellswood Park,
Torquay.**

As the chairman of the Haytor Traffic Group, I am in a position to be able to let you see 'Mr Wills' letter in its entirety. I am sure you will agree with me when I say that he is indeed a man of great vision and, like myself, is extremely fortunate to find an outlet for his not inconsiderable skills as an occasional contributor to the letters page of the *Mid-Devon Advertiser*.

2 Wellswood Park
Torquay TQ1 2QB
Tel: 01803 291 219

The Editor
Mid Devon Advertiser
Old Manor House
63 Wolborough Street
Newton Abbot TQ12 1NE

12th October 1996

Sir,

I am happy to be able to tell you that, responding to pressure from Environmentalists, the plans for a Motorway Spur to Widdecombe – which your paper has so often publicised – have been dropped. The idea of replacing the road with a railway was considered, but discarded, as rail travel is noisy, dirty, unhygenic, expensive and unreliable. Instead, an alternative, environmentally friendly solution has been adopted. It is planned to build a canal.

This magnificent construction will start at Stover, soar over Drumbridges roundabout on a viaduct, (with a spur to Trago to enable people to undertake environmentally friendly shopping), pass through Liverton and, in a series of some 50 to 80 locks, through Ilsington to Haytor. From there it will follow the line of the road to Harefoot Cross, where another series of locks will take it down to Widdecombe.

In order to preserve the environment, machinery will not be used to dig the canal. Instead there will be a force of 10,000 labourers with spades and wheelbarrows, creating much-needed employment in the West Country. In view of the contribution they have made to the debate, jobs will first be offered to road protesters, though it is feared they will be much too busy to have time to engage in gainful employment. The workforce will be housed in caravans, and one lane of the A38 will be closed so they can be parked there. Recreational facilities for the workforce – bingo halls, wine bars, bowling alleys, bordellos, etc – will be provided in temporary buildings on Liverton football ground.

As, when the canal is finished, it will take the best part of a day to get by barge from Stover to Haytor, and another day to get from there to Widdecombe and back, tourists will require overnight accommodation along the route. A new 300 bedroom hotel will be built on the site of the Haytor Car Park, with an eighteen hole golf course, racetrack, badminton court, and other environmentally friendly recreational facilities. The quarry at Haytor will be enlarged to provide a water supply for the canal, and there will be facilities there for sailing and scuba diving.

In times of drought, if the quarry cannot supply enough water, special tanker barges will fill up with water at Stover, make their way to Haytor, and release their loads so they can float down again to refill. In emergency, water will be brought by tanker up the road from Bovey Tracey, which will be widened to four lanes to accomodate the increased traffic.

When the construction is completed, much extra employment will have been created. There will be lock keepers, lock repairers, bargees, barge builders and repairers, hotel employees, and numerous ostlers, farriers, blacksmiths, grooms and so on to tend the horses who will pull the barges. (mechanically propelled boats will be banned). In order to accommodate these people, Haytor Vale will be designated as a New Town, with several thousand houses and an out-of-town shopping mall at Manaton.

Reached, of course, by canal.

It has been noted that people in Widdecombe who wish to go shopping, or to visit the doctor or dentist, will have to take two days over it instead of the two hours it takes at present. However, it was agreed that the improved environment would be good for them, and this outweighed the minor inconveniences to which they would be put.

If the scheme is successful, it is planned to replace the M5 with an Exeter to Bristol canal, and in time, it is hoped that the entire road system of the West Country will be replaced by waterways. This will ensure full employment in the region, with everyone spending their working lives moving other people slowly from place to place. The environment will be perfect, though the Region will not be prosperous. Its main industry, apart from barge transport, will be selling horse manure, but then, some of your correspondents are experts at that.

The ultimate environmental goal is, of course, to convert the Channel Tunnel into a canal for horse-drawn barges, with Heathrow and Gatwick as retirement homes for thousands of worn-out barge horses. There won't be many people left in Britain, but bees and bugs and butterflies will have a whale of a time ! Hooray !

Yours faithfully,

P.Wills

the party and thus they — the — just change the college...

Harken to this, Tom!

SIR: Yet another letter from Tom Widdicombe (October 4) prompted me to check the word Widdicombe in my Dietionary of Rare Words and Phrases, published by Pious and Trendman, 1995.

Widdicombe is a verb, both intransitive and transitive, and it means:

1 to pontificate from on high;

2 to make snide remarks, at irritatingly frequent intervals;

3 to flog a humorous notion to death.

The word exists, apparently, only in parts of Devon. It is not used elsewhere in the country.

PATRICK WILLETT,
72 East Street,
Ashburton.

'Take Moor Care' – a witticism!

SIR: I was fascinated indeed by Patrick Willets' letter (October 18) explaining the dictionary definition of the verb 'to widdicombe'.

I have to admit I have never come across the word used in that way myself, although in this area there is a similar word with a slightly changed spelling which is in quite common usage. It is interesting how, within such a small area, two such similar words can have such different meanings.

The phrase 'to be widecomed' is commonly applied to the coachloads of visitors to this area. It means to leave a place feeling lighter in the wallet, while clutching a chalk gnome or small toby jug.

A quick check in my thesaurus gives a couple of phrases of similar meaning: 'to be cheddar gorged', and, of more local interest, 'to be tragoed'.

While on the subject of words in local use, I must put on record my own feelings regarding the ongoing debate concerning the play on the word 'moor' on the numerous new signs throughout the national park.

As anyone who knows me will agree, I am normally a tolerant man, but listening to the gripes of my fellow middle-class pseudo-intellectuals moaning on about the use of this simple little pun is gradually beginning to get to me.

In my opinion, 'Take Moor Care' is a witticism of such depth and quality that whenever I see it I feel admiration welling up within me for the cleverness of its, as yet, anonymous creator.

As a resident within the park, I can genuinely assure you that the sentiment of this slogan is very close to my heart.

As for the size and garishness of the signs and road markings, as time passes by I am sure we will all grow to admire their inherent beauty, as indeed we have come to appreciate the usefulness of all those brown signs that so kindly warn us of the places that we should do our best to avoid.

All the best.

TOM WIDDICOMBE,
Woodlands,
Haytor Vale,
Newton Abbot.

9 Amberley Close
Holne CRoss
Ashburton
Newton Abbot TQ13 7JE

18 October 1996

Re 'Your Letters'

Reference letters from Messrs Widdicombe, Wills and Willett.(18.10.96)
Firstly Mr Wills states provisional plans for a motorway spur
to Widdicombe have been scrapped but this is not so as I have
contacted the D. of E. and their telephonist assured me they
were merely on hold (as are all brilliantly conceived and
innovdtive ideas received by govt. departments). However, the
concept of a canal from Stover to Widdecombe is breathtaking
in its simplicity and again full of innovations. I am sure
Mr Willett, having tired of the Spur road debate will be
eager to volunteer as the first among the 10.000 labourers
required to see the project through to completion.

Most importantly though, I believe Tom Widdecombe should
immediately set about co-opting P.Wills onto the Steering
Committee of the Haytor Traffic Group as working in harness,
their combined grasp of reality and abundant perception of the
environmental needs of the region will be of enormous benefit
to the community.

Yours faithfully

JOHN E. SKINNER
FOR THE MANY FRIENDS OF THE HAYTOR TRAFFIC GROUP

P.S. TO EDITOR
Thank you so much for printing letters of great humour which
I know cheer many people. Long may this policy continue
from your excellent publication.

Plans for spur are merely on hold...

SIR: Reference letters from Messrs Widdicombe, Wills and Willett (18.10.96).

First, Mr Wills states that provisional plans for a motorway spur to Widecombe have been scrapped, but this is not so. I have contacted the DoE and their telephonist assured me they were merely on hold (as are all brilliantly-conceived and innovative ideas received by government departments).

However, the concept of a canal from Stover to Widecombe is breathtaking in its simplicity and, again, full of innovations. I am sure Mr Willett, having tired of the spur road debate, will be eager to volunteer as the first among the 10,000 labourers required to see the project through to completion.

Most importantly, though, I believe Tom Widdicombe should immediately set about co-opting P. Wills on to the steering committee of the Haytor Traffic Group as, working in harness, their combined grasp of reality and abundant perception of the environmental needs of the region will be of enormous benefit to the community.

JOHN E. SKINNER,
For the many friends of
the Haytor Traffic Group.

9 Amberley Close,
Holne Cross,
Ashburton.

Woodlands
Haytor Vale   Tel: 01364 661470
Newton Abbot   Email: tom@mail.zynet.co.uk
Devon
TQ13 9XR

3rd November 96

Dear Mr Skinner

Thank you for the copy of your recently published letter
re your very welcome support for the Haytor Traffic
Group.

In due course I hope to actually hold an open meeting of
this now well known society to which of course you will
receive a special invitation. I am actually keen to get a
map drawn up of the area showing all the recently
proposed developments designed to ease our ever
worsening traffic problems. The map would also be
extremely useful for homeowners as it will clearly show
which properties will be severely blighted and more
seriously, those which will have to be demolished.

I am sure you were as delighted as I was to see that now
they are even beginning to discuss the possibility of
building a railway across the moor to relieve the strain on
the Dawlish sea wall. All we need now is a proposal for an
airport and we'll have the full set.

Many thanks for your support and long may good humour
prevail.

All the Best

Tom Widdicombe

The long-awaited map of the motorway system that will provide much-needed improvements to the lifestyle of the local populace.

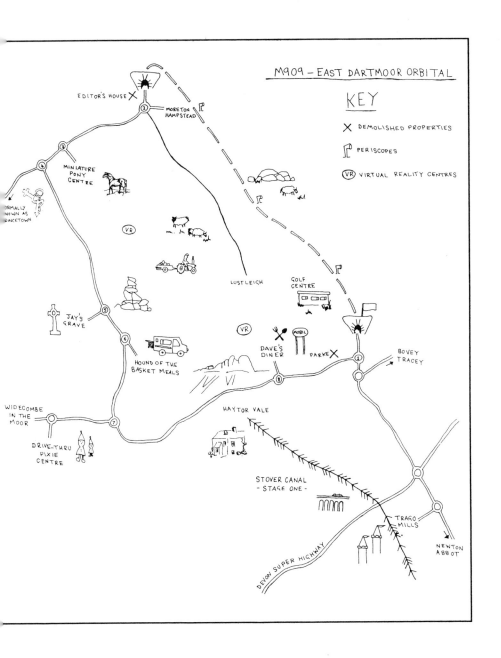

Tory conference disappointment

SIR: I imagine that your readers were as disappointed as I was to see that the highlight of this year's Tory conference was the proud presentation of their newest convert, local fisheries supremo Jim Portus.

As a member of the steering committee of the Haytor traffic group, I do feel in some way responsible for this rather surprising non-event. Despite intense pressure upon myself to sign up, I was unable to commit myself fully to the party and thus they were left with a desperate search for someone else of note to fulfil the demands of their conference schedule.

I must say that the promise of a comprehensive review of the Dartmoor orbital motorway system was a strong incentive to join, but in the end I really felt a move as big as joining a political party should be based on something more than achieving one's own immediate ends.

However, despite my hesitation, I must say how impressed I am with the upgrading of the A38 to an 'express superhighway'. For the cost of a couple of sheets of tin and a bit of signwriting, this has got to be good value.

Yes, real improvements, that is what this Government is all about. After all, it is so important that we perform well in the world league tables and we can surely rely on the Tories to halt the slide.

How do you increase the number of students getting A levels? Simple, make the exams easier.

How do you increase the number of university students? Simple, just change the colleges into universities. This is good, cost-effective government.

Imagine my surprise the other day to find that my second son, rarely seen out of bed before two in the afternoon, is now a student and no longer unemployed.

On closer examination, I find that he spends his time down the woods making paths and there is a Portakabin for him to go in if the weather turns bad.

One less on the unemployment statistics and one more on the number of students. Good stuff, eh!

TOM
WIDDICOMBE,
Woodlands,
Haytor Vale,
Newton Abbot.

Very amusing

SIR: I wish to comment on the letters from Tom Widdicombe, of Haytor Vale. I find them very amusing indeed, well written and with a good deal of satire.

The people who write in and criticise his letters have no sense of humour at all. I find some of his critics can only attack him personally.

I hope it does not put him off, which I don't think it would; he can rise above that. I just love his satire. Keep up the good work, Tom, and I look forward to reading your next letter.

                                        P. J. McCOURT,
Rora View,
Rora,
Liverton.

Advertiser/Post **Friday, December 25, 1996**

Tom refuses to ignore rubbish...!

SIR: I feel compelled to join the current debate in your letters page about the disposal of refuse in the Newton Abbot area. As regular readers will no doubt have realised, I have produced a considerable amount of rubbish myself over the years, and I am indeed greatly indebted to this journal for providing me with an outlet for the disposal of at least some of it.

Many times I have made the journey south of the A38 in an attempt to offload the seemingly endless supply of rubbish that my life creates.

Indeed, I myself have taken the long and winding road to the infamous Bickleigh Ball tip.

Once I even succeeded in dumping my load, only to be caught by a little man who promptly informed me that it was the wrong kind of rubbish.

I have to confess that, completely out of character, rather than reload the van I walked off and left him to it.

Of course, for the time being at least, rubbish disposal problems are a thing of the past as we have the excellent recycling facilities in Brunel Road.

Yes, if ever there were a candidate for one of John Major's famous 'charter marks' this yard is surely one. In fact, his best plan would surely be to dump the lot there and hope everyone forgets about the whole idea.

Whilst on the subject of rubbish, I see that Macdonalds are yet again over-riding the wishes of local people to supply us with the drive-through eating facility that our area so badly needs.

It is indeed refreshing that these large companies are able to crush local democracy almost at will in their efforts to provide us with cheap food.

Still, at least we don't have any rainforests they can destroy in the process.

In the immortal words of Ken Livingstone: 'If the vote had any power they would surely ban it'.

Happy Christmas.

TOM WIDDICOMBE,
Woodlands,
Haytor Vale,
Newton Abbot.

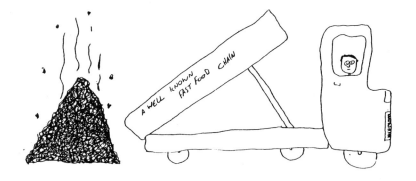

Tom reminds us that annual subs are due

SIR: Through the medium of your excellent journal, may I take the opportunity to remind your readers that the annual subscriptions to the Haytor Traffic Group are now due?

Perhaps I should also point out that full voting rights can only be enjoyed by fully paid-up members.

I am, of course, more than aware of the persistent undercurrent of dissatisfaction within the group during these difficult times.

Indeed, at one social gathering I attended over the festive season, I actually heard a remark suggesting that we were even less effective than the Conservative party when it comes to getting things done.

As you can imagine, I find this kind of cheap jibe particularly hurtful, but I must say it has made me more determined than ever to get at least one of our excellent projects off the ground in 1997.

On the plus side, I am sure the members will all be delighted to hear about the imminent purchase of a new 'Group van', bought with the aid of cash from the National Lottery and a substantial grant from the EEC.

It will, of course, be stained in dark oak and its primary function will be to get my shopping from Totnes once a week and to fetch the odd bale of hay for my horses.

Yes, real changes that make a real difference – that is what this organisation is all about.

So, as we approach the election, I must take this opportunity to warn the general public to be on their guard.

Watch out for hot air and empty promises.

Watch out for spurious statistics that prove nothing, especially when they are used as answers to difficult questions.

Let me make it clear from the start that, if I am re-elected as chairman of the HTG, I promise I will not put your interests before my own and I will definitely use my position of public responsibility to feather my own nest now and in the future.

Yes, you can rely on me to do what is right for Britain.

Have a happy, healthy and hopefully humourous New Year.

All the Best.

TOM WIDDICOMBE,
Woodlands,
Haytor Vale,
Newton Abbot.

New van,
New danger!

A NEW ROYAL YACHT...

Tom floats an opinion

SIR: As the chairman of the Haytor Traffic Group, can I say that I was more than a little surprised that I was not consulted on the future of the Royal Yacht project.

I cannot help wondering if this lack of consultation was just an unfortunate oversight on behalf of the Government, or was it a deliberate attempt to ignore my views on this important area of transport policy?

For the record, may I say here and now that, as a loyal citizen, nothing gives me greater pleasure than to give £60 million, (yes, £60,000,000) to build a new boat for Her Majesty to spend a couple of weeks a year on.

For goodness' sake, let's keep it in perspective.

The queen is, after all, one of the richest people in the world – one estimate puts the interest from her assets alone at £4 million a day – surely someone that rich deserves a new boat now and again?

I have heard some less loyal subjects ask why doesn't she buy her own boat?

After all, she wouldn't even notice £60 million being taken out of her bank account. And then we could use our £60 million to employ more doctors and nurses, and perhaps improve the facilities in our schools.

I can only sit back with sadness in my heart, when I think of the people that value these things above the basic necessities of Her Majesty.

If only I could convey to you in words how sad I was the day Windsor Castle caught fire etc, etc, etc.

All the best.

TOM WIDDICOMBE,
Woodlands,
Haytor Vale,
Newton Abbot.

Advertiser/Post **Friday, January 31, 1997**

The Royal Yacht

SIR: Surely – if the Royal Yacht cannot be economically repaired and a new one is needed, we must accept it.

The Royal Yacht does not only carry the Royals, I understand, but is an excellent advertisement to other countries of British workmanship that it visits.

We are so fortunate as a country in our Royal Family. I do think these 'professional grumblers' are becoming more boring – I wish they could take up knitting or gardening or some other occupation and not perpetually write with some moan or another to the Press!

**E. A. PATERSON,
54 Westcliff Road.
Dawlish.**

Tom's back on about The Beatles...!

SIR: I am in complete agreement with E. A. Paterson of Dawlish when he/she stated in last week's Letters Page that the 'professional grumblers' in our society have gone far enough.

For my part, I share the same sentiment about those people who constantly seek to find humour in the day-to-day affairs of our beloved country.

In these difficult times, with the millenium fast approaching and the proper funding still not in place, I am beginning to find it difficult to sleep at nights.

Add to this the almost constant mockery of the 'Cones Hotline', which I still believe to be one of John Major's greatest achievements, and it is no wonder people are getting annoyed.

And what about all the fuss caused by the selection of Alan Clark as the prospective Tory MP for Chelsea? Just because he bedded the two daughters of a High Court Judge, and then proceeded to do the same to their mother a few days later. He follows this up by telling us that he is totally devoted to his wife.

Let's face it, I'd be pretty devoted to my wife if she would let me get away with that kind of behaviour.

Of course, my favourite quote of the month was by one of the selection committee that chose Mr Clark as their candidate. He proudly announced: 'We just like the idea of having someone to represent us who owns 330,000 acres of our country.'

Now, that really is amusing, isn't it?

Yes, these are the people making all the important decisions for our nation and I am sure, like me, you can sleep more easily at night because of it.

How I long for the days before The Beatles, when leaning on your Triumph Herald, enjoying a good clean pun with your neighbour was considered to be 'having a jolly good laugh'.

If only we had known at the time the evil message behind the words 'She loves you, Yeah! Yeah! Yeah!', or, perhaps, the even more extreme 'I wanna hold your hand'.

Sadly, it is oh so easy to be wise after the event.

All the Best.

TOM WIDDICOMBE,
Woodlands,
Haytor Vale,
Newton Abbot.

Beware tunnellers!

SIR: Now that the Fairmile road protest has been brought to a successful conclusion, may I take this opportunity to warn the residents of South East Dartmoor, and especially the Wrey Valley, to be on their guard against tree-house dwellers and manic tunnellers.

I know you probably think that all this talk of motorway development in our area is most probably the product of an over-active mind, but we can never be too sure.

I do have it on good authority that the road protesters themselves are keen not to be wrong-footed on this one and are ready to dig in at a moment's notice.

It is all too easy to sit back and let others do the worrying. Before you know where you are, you will be surrounded by anarchic revolutionaries with nothing less than the future of the planet on their minds.

If you want to stand up for the British way of life and fight for the future of the motor car, then join me now.

The sooner our country is completely covered in concrete the better. Let them try and tunnel through that, that's what I say.

MRS CYNTHIA CORNFLAKE
(Name and address supplied)

Could we cope with Tom being cloned?

SIR: Following the recent breakthrough in the sheep cloning project, I have some excellent news to share with your readers.

Within hours of the success being announced through the media, I received an important phone call from the prominent government scientist, Sir Ivor Test-Tube, in which he outlined a last-ditch plan that, hopefully, will avoid the election of a much-feared Labour Government in a few weeks' time.

I must say that I am still finding this hard to believe but I can assure you, hand on heart, that this is not just the wild imagination of an old hippy's mind, shot to ribbons by excess living.

As you must all be aware, time is running out and New Danger is almost upon us. The importance of this matter cannot be overstated and, unless we can start another Falklands war double quick, this is our only hope.

Here is the plan. I am being taken into a top secret laboratory where I will be cloned, and shortly there will be an exact replica of me in every constituency in the country.

Yes, 630 identical beings, the same as me in every detail, will shortly be released around the entire country.

Of course, my first question (but probably not yours) is 'Why me?'

Apparently, I have been selected because of my obvious belief in good old-fashioned values, and my constant efforts to improve the traffic systems in and around Haytor.

Also, my unstinting support for, and belief in, the Cones Hotline which has done so much to improve the quality of life for so many of us throughout the UK — the homeless and the single mothers spring to mind.

As you can imagine, I am greatly honoured to be selected in this way, but at the same time I am also a little apprehensive. Designing a tunnel through the Wrey valley is one thing - saving the country from

New Danger is quite another.

Your support, as always, will be greatly appreciated and, as ever, I can promise you that my own self-interest is paramount.

Your humble servant,
TOM WIDDICOMBE,
Woodlands,
Haytor Vale,
Newton Abbot.

Advertiser/Post **Friday, March 7, 1997**

Pension increase – could Tom Widdicombe help?

SIR: My wife and I are over the moon, we feel that we have won the lottery!

April will see an increase in the water rate by £8.16 per annum and an increase in the council tax of £38.49 per annum. Through the generosity of the Government, our old age pension rises by £131.86 per annum.

We will be £1.63 per week 'better off', except we have not taken into account the rise on TV Licence, road fund licence or the rise in petrol, which automatically puts the price of goods up in the shops.

We are so thrilled with our 'windfall' and am appealing to your readers as to where best to invest this 'vast amount'.

Perhaps Mr Tom Widdicombe may be able to help!!

LES HAMBLETON,

4 Broadpark,
Bovey Tracey.

Woodlands
Haytor Vale   Tel: 01364 661470
Newton Abbot   Email:106770.3311@compuserve
Devon
TQ13 9XR

13th April 97

Dear Mr Hambleton

I am indeed honoured that you have asked me for advice
regarding the, in my opinion, rather excessive rise in your
pension.

I fear my reply through the letters page of the Mid Devon has
come a cropper because of the impending election. However I
am enclosing a copy for you personally and I hope you find it of
some amusement.

Thank you for your support and long may humour survive as
the most effective weapon in the armoury of the people.

All the Best

Tom Widdicombe

*Oh Tom
ye of little faith*

Nothing fazes George!

Tom advises on how to eke out that pension

SIR: After much thought, I have decided that I can indeed offer what I hope will be some useful advice to Mr Hambleton on how best to survive on his pension. (Letter: Pension increase – could Tom Widdicombe help?)

Although I am not a qualified financial advisor, is it not by chance that I have amassed a vast personal fortune.

My secret is good old-fashioned hard work, combined with an astute business brain – yes, these are the qualities that have taken me to the top.

One thing I feel I must say straight away, however, is that it is a long time since I have had to deal with such paltry amounts of money as those you are talking about. I actually think your best option is perhaps to concentrate on cutting expenditure, and it is in this area that I think I can be of some help to you.

Only this week we had a friend over for dinner and he was accompanied by his new girl-friend from Totnes.

I know it is hard to believe, but I swear to God this is true, she brought with her a bag of stinging nettles which she steamed for a few minutes before putting some on all of our plates.

She also provided a bowl of 'salad stuff', which included such delicacies as primrose flowers, tender bramble shoots, ground elder, and numerous other bits and pieces picked from the hedgerows.

Obviously, there could be huge savings here for pensioners and, of course, it would also save enormous sums of money currently spent by the council on weed control.

The picture in my mind of crowds of elderly people happily grazing on the verges of our roads is surely a vision for the future well worth considering.

Another simple idea that I think would work well is to take a hessian sack and cut a slit in the end, big enough to get your head through, and a slit on each side for your arms.

This will give you a perfectly acceptable garment which, I think, will keep you very warm throughout the year.

If you find it difficult to get hold of a hessian sack, you could use a paper animal feed bag instead – you can pick one up at any farm – these would be fine in dry weather.

You can also wrap newspaper around your legs and tie it on with baler twine, but don't tie it too tight as it may cut off your probably already-failing circulation. It is surprising how quickly you will be able to adjust the tension of the twine to perfection.

Little ideas like these can literally save you pounds over the years and I am sure that, in the true spirit of the enterprise economy, you will quickly discover the joys of survival in this ever-more efficient and cost-effective society.

If you have any problems getting hold of feed bags or baler twine, please let me know and I'll drop some down for you.

All the best,

TOM WIDDICOMBE,
Woodlands,
Haytor Vale.

With tongue firmly in cheek!

SIR: In the next few weeks, the British people have the opportunity to choose a new government.

I do hope that this newspaper will not be following the *Sun* by coming out in favour of New Danger just because they can't bear to be on the losing side.

There really is a lot more at stake here than just selling a few papers — this is after all, about the future of our great nation.

As an example, look at what I personally could lose if we end up with Tony 'red eyes' Blair in charge.

Daddy says that it will almost certainly be the end of my positions on two hospital quangos that he managed to organise for me. (I do so hate that work quango — it reminds me of a disastrous affair I once had with one of our builders).

It has been so handy over the last few years getting £200 a week for doing virtually nothing. And that is just me — there are going to be hundreds of us, all having to fall back on our family fortunes until we can get back into power again.

Mind you, Daddy says not to worry too much because they will only be in govern-ment for five years, and that they are so right wing now that we will hardly notice the difference anyway.

All the same, we should all think very hard about the pros and cons before we cast our votes.

As the daughter of a politician I do find elections so exciting. But I do hope Daddy doesn't lose his seat — he gets so cross when he has to pay for all his own meals, and he does so love all those free trips abroad.

Good Hunting!

CYNTHIA CORNFLAKE (Mrs),
(Address supplied).

Advising the Editor...!

SIR: Although there are conventionally good reasons for Editors to allow correspondents to their letters' pages to use pen names and/or to have their addresses withheld, it does seem to an avid reader that you are being unduly and increasingly generous in this respect.

It is hard to see why it was possible for 'Observer' to write an overtly political letter on March 27, or for 'Ramroaster' to complain on April 4 that businesses prefer to use an address of Newton Abbot rather than Kingsteignton, without disclosing their respective names and addresses.

This letter was particularly odd as the complaint was so innocuous, while Mr Ballamy's courageous letter, printed immediately below, was clearly identified.

You also published on April 4 a letter without an address from 'Cynthia Cornflake' which may have been amusing, but was also highly political, probably insulting, and possibly libellous.

Surely the authors of such letters, which neither cover public concerns nor present any risk to the writers, should be expected to be identified and not to be shielded by anonymity; perhaps you could set out for us sceptics your criteria in this field?

**P. E. HART,
Little Moretons,
Combeinteignhead.**

● See rider at end of 'Observer's' letter this week. Agreed, Cynthia Cornflake's letter was highly-political, we are in the run-up to a General Election, after all. Had it been libellous, it would not have been published. Editor.

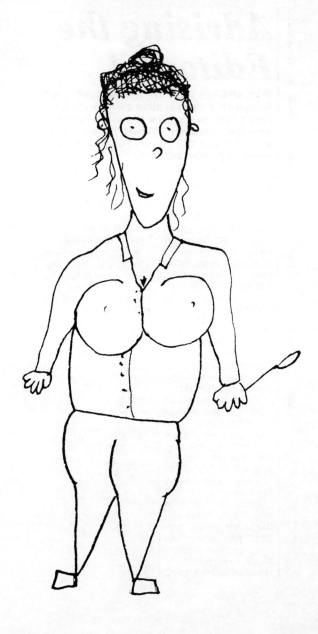

Artist's impression of Cynthia Cornflake

*. . and of her
one-time lover*

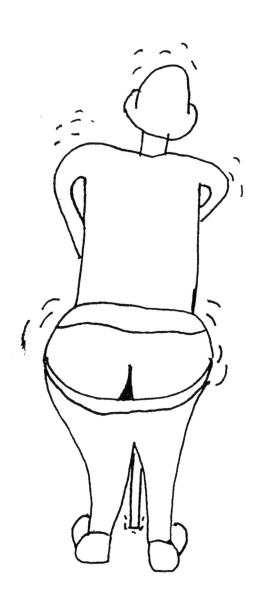

Haytor traffic keeps Tom away from Parliament

SIR: I am more than aware of the devastation and disappointment caused by my decision not to contest the Teignbridge seat in the forthcoming election.

May I put the record straight once and for all: my decision has nothing whatsoever to do with the fact that I might lose my deposit.

As the self-appointed chairman of the HTG (Haytor Traffic Group), I am wholeheartedly committed to solving the problems of traffic in and around the Haytor area. I have taken on this commitment and I intend to see it through.

Representing the people of Teignbridge in parliament, although obviously a great honour, would surely distract me from my main task, the urgency of which is apparent for all to see.

I know many people will think that this is a chance lost, but, truthfully, traffic is my first love. Since I was a child, it has been my dream to mastermind an efficient transport system and it would surely be wrong to abandon my plans now that they are so close to fruition.

Thank you all for your support and I hope I will not be quite so busy in the year 2002.

All the best

TOM WIDDICOMBE,
Woodlands,
Haytor Vale,
Newton Abbot.

PS. I have checked in the 'phone book and with directory enquiries and there is no such surname as Cornflake. Either she is not on the phone or, as Mr Hart suggests, that is indeed not her real name. One way or another I will track her down — she sounds like my kind of woman!

PPS

SIR: Re Letters Page, April 25, 1997, concerning the postscriptum to Tom Widdicombe's letter.

Might I suggest he goes out in 'force' to find the lady with the unlikely name?

She was, I believe, at one time to be seen in the imaginings of Sir Arthur Conan Doyle – but that was many years ago, even before Jetty Marsh Road.

Let us hope Tom will soon dicover the lady's whereabouts, or I fear we are in for yet another protracted serial!

JIM MILLS,
8 Gladstone Place,
Newton Abbot.

PS. If the word 'force' fails to ring a bell, you may be younger than you think!

Mr T. Widdicombe

Woodlands

Haytor Vale

Newton Abbot

DEVON

1997

Tempora labuntur, tacitis senescimus
annis... [Ov.]

Fratres: Hora est iam nos de somno
surgere... [Rom. 13, 11]

Respondit Thomas et dixit ei:
Dominus meus et Deus meus. [Joh. 20,28]

ALIENA OPTIMUM FRUI INSANIA

VITA SINE PROPOSITIO VAGA EST

SEMPER RESPICE FINEM

SUPRA OMNIA

NIL ILLEGITEMI CARBORUNDUM.

[Tom 1, 1]

I know it's hard to believe
But YES
They chose them in this order:

**Patrick
Nicholls**

**24,679
votes**

**Richard
Younger-Ross**

**24,398
votes**

**Sue
Dann**

**11,311
votes**

If only Sir Ivor had completed the operation in time, we would not
now be facing the prospect of ten long years of New Danger

Now, the consequences...

SIR: What a sad day for Britain and the Empire. Our beloved Conservative Party has suffered utter humiliation at the hands of the electorate.

Of course, the good news in Teignbridge is that 'Our Pat' has managed to hang on in there and will be representing us all at Westminster for another five years. I can't help thinking what a difference it would have made if a few of those 817 Greens had voted tactically.

Sadly, the scientists slipped behind schedule on my cloning operation and, alas, without my much-needed help, the seats around the rest of the country just fell like ninepins.

Now we have to live with the consequences. Smaller class sizes for a start — does anything make you more angry? Less VAT on fuel, that's only going to benefit the poor isn't it?

And now they are talking about closing the tax loopholes that the rich have been exploiting since time began. Whatever next! Yes, after eighteen glorious years, it really looks like our number is up. In a strange kind of way, I feel a huge sense of relief that it is now all over and we can all forget about politics for the foreseeable future.

For myself, I have decided to devote my energies to tracking down the ever more elusive Mrs Cynthia Cornflake, and I am indeed grateful to Mr Jim Mills for encouraging me to get on with the task as quickly as possible.

In line with Jim's pun-ridden evidence, I can confirm that there was indeed a family of Cornflakes living in this area long before Jetty Marsh Road was even a planner's dream.

Alas, there the trail seems to end and I can only appeal to the readers of this auspicious journal to help me in my search.

Of course, if Cynthia herself would like to respond to my pleas, then that would make my world complete.

TOM WIDDICOMBE,
Woodlands,
Haytor Vale,
Newton Abbot.

A crisp response...

SIR: I must say that I am very surprised by the constant speculation in the letters pages about the origins and present day whereabouts of the Cornflake family.

I do, of course, feel honoured by the interest in this subject, although I must say straightaway, I myself am only a Cornflake through marriage. In fact, I married the last surviving male member of the family and it was our great hope that we could indeed carry on the noble name.

Sadly, this was not to be and in some despair, my husband Barry rather let his standards slip. In fact, I have not seen him for several years. I have now come to accept that I am the sole surviving Cornflake in this area, if not the entire country.

I don't know about anyone else, but I am having serious doubts about the true political beliefs of the all-too-often heard, Mr Tom Widdicombe.

Of course, I am flattered by his willingness to meet me, but I remain unconvinced by the style of his writing.

Sometimes I feel that I might even be the target of his humour and, if that is the case, I think it would be hard for me to trust and like a man like that.

After the trauma of the election, and what with Daddy losing his seat as well, I feel like I really cannot face any more disappointment in my life at the moment.

Yet, at the same time, despite his politics, I feel compelled to reveal my whereabouts to, and also to meet, Tom Widdicombe, if only to tell him to stop writing so many of his absurd letters to our beloved local newspaper.

CYNTHIA CORN-FLAKE (Mrs), (name and address supplied)

Tom has denied a link with the lottery

SIR: Yet again, I am having to use the columns of your illustrious journal to put the record straight once and for all. I can categorically state that there is no truth in the rumour that the 84 per cent rise in my income last week is in any way connected to the massive share dividends received by the 'fatcat' Winalot lottery directors at the same time.

When I took over as chairman of the Haytor Traffic Group, I made clear in my contract that should I wish to take up the options on my share allocation, I could do so at any time.

No-one has worked harder than I to make the group a success, and surely my achievements so far are not in question?

I have no qualms at all about taking the cash now, although I do have to admit that I am somewhat surprised by the amount of profit I have made.

Accordingly, I have decided to contribute an undisclosed percentage of these profits to a charity of my choice, in the hope that I can limit the damage caused to my already severely-dented image.

This decision has nothing to with the threat from the Government to close down the HTG on the grounds that it is no longer funny, and is now no more than a desperate attempt to get a cheap laugh.

I hope that this has clarified the situation. I have said many times before that the HTG exists solely for my benefit, and the fact that some people have found it a source of amusement over the past few months is surely just a bonus.

Quite frankly, how anyone can find humour in the traffic situation around Haytor Vale is beyond me.

All the best.

TOM WIDDICOMBE,
Woodlands,
Haytor Vale.

The end of an era

In a rare moment of frankness, I must tell you that I was truly touched when I first read Cynthia's last letter. What is it that brings about that magical moment when you realise that you are on the verge of something very special indeed?

I decided, there and then, that despite my present situation and everything that has gone on so far in my life, this was a feeling too strong to ignore. I knew in my heart of hearts that I was playing for high stakes - my family, my vast wealth, and perhaps most importantly my standing in the local community, but somehow all this paled into insignificance compared to the prospect of coming face to face with Cynthia.

There seemed to be an overpowering force pulling us together. Against the not inconsiderable power of my logic urging extreme caution, I launched myself into the unknown.

*　　*　　*

We arranged to meet for tea at a cafe near Cynthia's home. When I first saw her my heart sank. It's the jodhs that I can't get out of my mind - they really said it all. However, if Cynthia was a disappointment to me, it was as nothing compared to the disappointment that I was to her. Through the weeks of speculation and gossip in the press about my interest in her and her family, she had built up her hopes beyond all reason. Cynthia had turned me into a fantasy figure destined to satisfy her every need. This was mission impossible for me, even had I been willing - sadly, on meeting Cynthia, I was not. For the first few minutes I desperately tried to lower her expectations whilst looking for a way out of what had every chance of becoming a very difficult situation.

Meanwhile Cynthia, blinded by her dreams, was coming on strong and I was beginning to panic. The last thing I needed right then, or at any other time for that matter, was to get involved with a lady who I was rapidly diagnosing as seriously dangerous to my well-being.

From there things went downhill fairly swiftly. I began to get a very clear picture of her plans; rather worryingly, she did not begin to get a picture of my inability to fulfil them. Cynthia had her future all mapped out and, unbelievably, I was down to play a major part in it. I slammed myself into reverse gear and put my foot hard on the gas pedal - it was all a bit too close to home to be funny.

Then, out of the blue, she leant towards me. I'll remember these words forever. She said, "Of course, you'll have to give me a few days, I've got to move that builder on. He keeps coming back like a bad penny."

That was enough for me. I'm not one to miss a chance when I'm up against the wall. "Cynthia, I don't believe I'm hearing this. If that's how you treat your men I'm afraid you're not for me."

We left each other with no plans to meet again. For me, it was more than enough to know that Cynthia Cornflake really does exist and is not, as so many people have told me, simply the product of some desperate character out there trying to be funny.

Cynthia,
doing what she
loves doing
most...

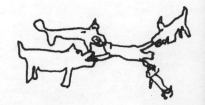

I warned against eco-warriors...

SIR: I have to say that I have no sympathy at all with WBB clay company. In my first letter to this newspaper, back in February of this year, I clearly warned everyone to be on their guard for eco-warrior invasions, and now they have struck and, if I may say so, right where it hurts.

For the sake of a few wretched kingfishers these idealists are prepared to jeopardise the nation's entire production of lavatory pans, on which our happiness so depends.

This is nothing less than a cynical attack on the soft underbelly of our society and, as such, deserves the contempt of us all.

Surely even these desperate people realise how difficult life would be without what can only be described as these absolute necessities?

As usual, these young idealists have not considered the full consequences of their actions and the shortage of such vital earthenware over the next few years can surely only damage the environmental cause.

In the short term, I have more than enough to worry about without having to live in dread of accidentally cracking my pan on a dark winter's night.

Right now, with the cubbing season coming up and the young hounds desperately in need of tasting blood, I really could do without this extra worry. Sometimes I really do wonder if all this modern education is doing more harm than good!

Let's enjoy the hunting season while we jolly well can, eh!

CYNTHIA CORNFLAKE.

Make HTG a bank and enjoy the windfall

SIR: I am more than a little surprised at the negative response that I have received to the proposal that the Haytor Traffic Group should become a bank. This proposal, if accepted by the membership at the AGM, wil be a significant turning point in the already illustrious history of this vibrant organisation.

As the chairman of HTG, it is my duty to point out to you, the members, the huge single advantage of voting in favour of this change. That is, of course, the huge wad you will receive in return for your share of what has hitherto been a mutual society.

Like you, I am of course very proud of what we have achieved over the years, but you must understand that in this ever more competitive world it is vital that we are able to compete on equal terms with other traffic groups. To be left behind now, as we approach the millenium, would, I can assure you, leave me with a feeling of deep personal failure and regret from which I am not sure I could ever fully recover.

Since that glorious day in 1979 when Mrs Thatcher set about making Britain Great again, I have given my all to the many changes that we have all had to face up to. I have gone out there to make money regardless; I have accepted that there is no such thing as society; I have bought a mobile 'phone and I have installed an Aga in my kitchen. But, above all this, and through nothing less than sheer hard work and dedication, I have become the chairman of the Haytor Traffic Group.

Yes, I would like the young people of today to look on me as an example of what can be achieved in today's classless society. Of course I have had to make sacrifices along the way – I well remember those long summer evenings at home with my books while my friends, without a care in the world, were off listening to their Beatles records....

TOM WIDDICOMBE,
Woodlands,
Haytor Vale,
Newton Abbot.

Advertiser/Post **Friday, September 12, 1997**

The new Haytor Traffic Group logo was designed, with no expense spared, by top 90s designer, Sir Terence Conman, working alongside top 90s PR guru, Sir Tim Bull.

The logo encapsulates the dynamic times that we live in and will, without doubt, go a long way towards establishing our new corporate image. (so important these days, don't you think?)

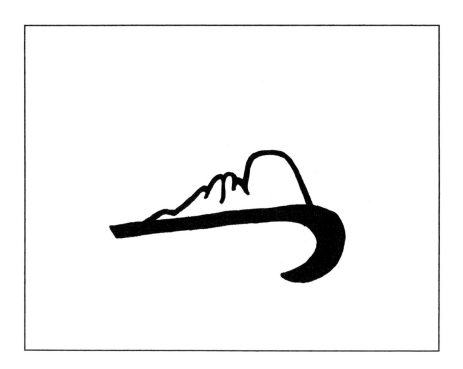

_ _ _ _ _ _ tcar here and knock 50% off the value of this highly collectable book_ _ _ _ _ _ _ _ _

To the directors of Haytor Traffic Group

I agree wholeheartedly with the proposal to turn Haytor Traffic Group into a Bank. My opinion has in no way been influenced by the huge amount of dosh that I will be receiving for doing absolutely nothing.
Please send me the cheque as soon as possible.

signed: